Teacher Jokes
for kids

First published in Great Britain 1988 by Ward Lock Limited,
8 Clifford Street, London W1X 1RB, an Egmont company.

This edition published 2004 by Bounty Books,
a division of Octopus Publishing Group Ltd,
2-4 Heron Quays, London E14 4JP
Reprinted 2004, 2005

ISBN 0 7537 0881 7
ISBN 13 9780753708811

Printed and bound in Dubai

Teacher Jokes
for kids

Bounty
Books

What's the difference between a headmaster and a packet of toffees?
    People like toffees.

What did one maths book say to the other?
    'Boy, have I got problems!'

When Steve and Smart Alec were playing football, Steve made a shot at the goal, which went wide. 'I could kick myself,' he moaned.
    'Don't bother,' said Alec, 'you'd only miss.'

Which animals do you have to beware of when taking exams?
   Cheetahs.

What takes a lot of licks from a teacher without complaint?
   An ice-cream.

Mrs Smith: 'What position does your Jimmy have in the school football team?'
Mrs Jones: 'I think he's one of the drawbacks.'

Smart Alec's brother had a new teacher.
   'And does the teacher like you?' asked his mum.
   'I think so,' he replied. 'She puts kisses on all my sums.'

Smart Alec had a week off school with 'flu. When he returned, his teacher politely asked him how he felt.

'With my hands,' he replied.

Smart Alec's class were doing a project about North American animals.

'Please, Miss,' began Darren, 'is it true that a bear won't harm you if you carry a piece of cheese in your pocket?'

Before the teacher could reply, Smart Alec called out, 'It depends how fast you carry it!'

Science teacher: 'Who created the London Underground?'
Clever Clara: 'Moles, Miss?'

Who wrote Good Behaviour in School?
    Emma Prefect.

Music teacher: 'Now who can tell me the name of their favourite musical instrument?'
Smart Alec: 'The dinner bell, Miss.'

Who invented fractions?
Henry 1/8.

The first form were being taught to say Grace before school dinner, but Jonathan didn't join in. 'Now, Jonathan,' said his teacher, 'don't you say a prayer before dinner at home?'
    'No, Miss,' replied Jonathan. 'My mum can cook.'

Sally: 'Which animals are best at maths?'
Susie: 'Rabbits, because they multiply so well.'
Sally: 'Rabbits might multiply, but only a snake can be an adder.'

Did you hear about the cross-eyed teacher? She couldn't control her pupils.

Why is history like a fruit cake?
    Because it's full of dates.

Ben: 'Are slugs nice to eat, Miss?'
Teacher: 'Don't be so disgusting, Ben. Eat up your dinner and be quiet.'
Teacher (later): 'Now, what was that you were asking, Ben?'
Ben: 'It was about slugs, Miss. But it's too late now. You had one on your plate, but it's gone.'

Teacher: 'Why are you late this morning?'
Robin: 'Please, Miss, I was dreaming about a Manchester United match.'
Teacher: 'But why did that make you late?'
Robin: 'They had extra time.'

Why did Henry VIII have so many wives?
Because he liked to chop and change.

Teacher: 'Why are you standing in front of the mirror with your eyes closed?'
Rosie: 'So I can see what I look like when I'm asleep.'

Teacher: 'Where does your mother come from, Matthew?'
Matthew: 'Alaska.'
Teacher: 'Don't bother, I'll ask her myself.'

GULP! CAN'T WE HAVE A DOPEY TEACHER!

Teacher: 'Name six things that contain milk.'
Daft Dora: 'Custard, cocoa and four cows.'

Teacher: 'How do you make a fire with two sticks?'
Smart Alec: 'Make sure one of the sticks is a match.'

Biology teacher: 'Can anyone tell me what kind of creature a slug is?'
Smart Alec: 'I'd say it was a snail with a housing problem.'

Teacher: 'Don't shuffle your feet when you walk into assembly. Pick them up.'
Small voice from the back: 'When we've picked them up, should we carry them in our satchels?'

French teacher: 'Who can tell me what the French national anthem is called?'
Cuthbert: 'The *Mayonnaise*, Miss.'

What do French children say at the end of their school dinners?
    'Mercy.'

Why did King Arthur have a round table?
    So no one could corner him.

English teacher: 'This term we're going to study Kipling. Do you like Kipling, Brenda?'
Brenda: 'I don't know, Miss. I've never kippled.'

Mum: 'Samantha, you came bottom out of ten in maths!'

Samantha: 'Yes, Mum, but it could have been much worse.'

Mum: 'How?'

Samantha: 'I could have been in Sarah's group and come bottom out of twenty.'

Dad: 'Did you get a good place in your exams?'

Donald: 'Oh, yes. I sat next to the school swot.'

Jeremy was slouching in his chair with his feet stuck out in the aisle, chewing gum in the middle of a history lesson. The teacher called, 'Jeremy, take that gum out of your mouth and put your feet in this instant!'

David, on the phone: 'Our David has a bad cold and can't come to school today.'
Teacher: 'I'm sorry to hear that. To whom am I speaking?'
David: 'This is my father.'

Why did the teacher put wheels on her rocking chair?
    She liked to rock and roll.

Did you hear about the boy who was told to do 100 lines? He drew 100 cats on the paper, because he thought the teacher had said 'lions'.

Latin is a language
Dead as it can be.
First it killed the Romans
And now it's killing me.

Maths teacher: 'Add 4911 to 3748, divide by 3, and multiply by 7. What have you got?'
Mary: 'The wrong answer.'

What do you call a teacher with two lavatories on her head?
      Lulu.

Maths teacher: 'What are 3 times 7?'
James: '21.'
Maths teacher: 'Good!'
James: 'Good? It was perfect!'

Cathy: 'I've added this sum up ten times, Miss.'
Teacher: 'Well done, Cathy.'
Cathy: 'And here are my ten answers.'

Dad: 'Shall I help you with your homework?'
Son: 'No thanks, I'd rather get it
wrong by myself.'

*What do you call a
teacher who has spots?*
  Dot.

Maths teacher: 'If you had £7.47p in one pocket, and £4.26p in the other pocket, what would you have?'
Smart Alec: 'Someone else's trousers on!'

Maths teacher: 'If I had seven oranges in this hand, and nine oranges in this hand, what would I have?'
Cuthbert: 'Big hands, Sir.'

Smart Alec's class was doing a project about milk. Everyone wrote several pages about how milk came from cows, and was taken to dairies in tankers, and bottled, then delivered to our doorstep by the milkman. But Smart Alec's project was only three lines long. He explained that he'd written about condensed milk.

Visitor to school: 'Why is that boy locked in a cage in a corner of the classroom?'
Bertha: 'That's Neville. He's the teacher's pet.'

Casper asked Jasper what his favourite school subject was. Jasper replied, 'Gozinta.'

'What do you mean, 'gozinta'?' asked Casper.

'You know,' replied Jasper. 'Two gozinta four, four gozinta eight...'

Smart Alec's class was being very naughty, with everyone shouting at once. The teacher called out, 'Be quiet when you're talking to me!'

How do you make a stupid teacher laugh at the end of term?
　　Tell her a joke at the start of term.

If you have a referee in football, and an umpire in cricket, what do you have in bowls?
　　Goldfish.

Teacher: 'Martin, put some more water in the fish tank, please.'
Martin: 'But they haven't drunk the water I gave them yesterday, Sir.'

Teacher: 'Andrew, your homework looks as if it's in your father's handwriting.'
Andrew: 'Well, I used his pen, Sir.'

Silly Sue was told to write a composition about the Andes for her homework. She began, 'The Andes can be found at the end of the armies...'

Tracy: 'Would you punish someone for something they hadn't done?'
Teacher: 'Of course not.'
Tracy: 'Good, because I haven't done my homework.'

What do you call a teacher with a paper bag on his head?
Russell.

Did you hear about the class of children from a city school who went for a ramble in the country? They found a crate of empty milk bottles and thought they'd discovered a cow's nest!

English teacher: 'Did you write this poem, Emily?'
Emily: 'Yes, Miss.'
English teacher: 'Well, I'm very pleased to meet you, Robert Browning.'

Dave: 'The trouble with our teachers is that they all do bird impressions.'
Mave: 'Really? What do they do?'
Dave: 'They watch us like hawks.'

Carol: 'I'm going to read my poem aloud. *There was a young lady named Nellie, Who went into the sea up to her knees...*'
Daryl: 'That's not a poem. It doesn't rhyme.'
Carol: 'I know, but that's because she didn't wade out far enough.'

'Our teacher is amazing. He's about ninety years old and hasn't got a grey hair on his head.'
    'Really?'
    'Yes, in fact he's completely bald.'

Doreen: 'Yesterday for dinner we had Enthusiasm Stew.'
Maureen: 'What's Enthusiasm Stew?'
Doreen: 'It's when the cook puts everything she's got into it.'

When are school sausages noisy?
    When they're bangers.

When Smart Alec complained that the chicken pie tasted funny, he was told it was no laughing matter.

How long is school spaghetti cooked?
    About thirty centimetres.

Geography teacher: 'What makes the Leaning Tower of Pisa lean?'
Smart Alec: 'Nobody feeds it.'

THAT'S WHERE THEY MAKE THOSE ROUND THINGS YOU EAT!

Geography teacher: 'What is a Laplander?'
Smart Alec: 'Someone who's not very good at standing on a crowded bus.'

One teacher wanted to know why Jenny had written that the people of the USSR were very energetic. 'Well, Miss,' replied Jenny, 'they're Russian here, Russian there...'

Simple Simon was writing a geography essay. It began, 'The people who live in Paris are called parasites...'

What was the largest island in the world before Australia was discovered?
    Australia.

The pupils of the sixth form, who had learned to type, were being interviewed by prospective employers. Lisa was asked her typing speed.

'I'm not sure,' she replied, 'but I can delete at fifty words a minute.'

Teacher: 'I want to talk to you about energy conservation. Who can give me an example of energy being wasted?'
Smart Alec: 'Telling a hair-raising story to a bald man.'

Science teacher: 'Can anyone tell me what nitrates are?'
Smart Alec: 'Well, they must be dearer than day rates, Sir.'

When Smart Alec was asked to write an essay on cricket, he handed in a piece of paper with just two words written on it. They were: *I'm stumped.*

Teacher: 'Ronald, why are you late for school?'
Ronald: 'I sprained my ankle, Miss.'
Teacher: 'What a lame excuse.'

Jim: 'Let's sell our teachers and make some money.'

Tim: 'But who would buy them?'

Jim: 'I don't know, but I heard on the news that Old Masters fetch very good prices these days.'

What do you do with a wombat?
    Play wom.

Teacher: 'Florence, you look very pale this morning. Are you all right?'

Florence: 'Yes, Miss, but I gave my face a good wash.'

What do kangaroos have that no other animal has?
    Baby kangaroos.

Why is school like a shower?
   One wrong turn and you're in hot water.

What happened when the teacher's dog swallowed a roll of film?
   Nothing serious developed.

Why did Ken keep his trumpet in the fridge?
   Because he liked cool music.

English teacher: 'Alec, were you copying Ralph's work?'

Smart Alec: 'No, I was just checking that he'd got mine right.'

English teacher: 'Raymond, please do not hum while reading your English book.'

Raymond: 'I'm not reading, Sir, just humming.'

Alice: 'Did your music teacher say you had a heavenly voice?'

Aileen: 'Not really. She said it was like nothing on earth.'

'Marion, it's time for your cello lessons.'
   'Oh, fiddle!'

Dad: 'Susan, why has your teacher banned you from cookery lessons?'

Susan: 'I, um, burnt something.'

Dad: 'That doesn't sound very serious.'

Susan: 'The teachers thought it was. It was the school kitchen.'

'Dad, Dad, I need a new pair of shorts for gym.'
'Why can't Jim buy his own shorts?'

Why did the teacher switch on the lights?
Because her pupils were so dim.

History teacher: 'Alec, can you tell me what nationality Napoleon was?'
Smart Alec: 'Corsican!'

What was King Arthur's favourite game?
Knights and crosses.

Why is tennis such a noisy game?
Because every player raises a racket.

School doctor: 'I'm afraid your son needs glasses.'
Parent: 'How can you tell?'
School doctor: 'By the way he came in through the window.'

Parent to school doctor: 'I think my daughter has flat feet. Can you give her something?'
School doctor: 'How about a bicycle pump?'

Why is Europe like a frying pan?
   Because it has Greece at the bottom.

What does a teacher have that her class doesn't have?
   The answers.

History teacher: 'Napoleon was defeated at Waterloo. As a matter of fact, one of my ancestors died at Waterloo.'
Jamie: 'Really, Miss? Which platform?'

Teacher: 'What can you tell me about Moses?'
Polly: 'He wore a wig, Miss.'
Teacher: 'What makes you think that?'
Polly: 'Because sometimes he was seen with Aaron and sometimes without.'

Kevin: 'I see you're wearing your Easter tie.'
Keith: 'Why do you call it my Easter tie?'
Kevin: 'Because it's covered in egg.'

What did the school tie say to the school beret?
  'You go on ahead, while I hang around.'

The school caretaker was mopping the floor in the corridor.

'I say!' shouted Smart Alec. 'Your bucket doesn't look very well.'

'What are you talking about?' grumbled the caretaker.

'Your bucket doesn't look well to me,' replied Smart Alec. 'In fact it looks a little pale.'

The maths teacher was telling his class about his life in Australia before he became a teacher.

'I used to chase after kangaroos on horses,' he said proudly.

'Coo, I didn't know kangaroos could ride horses!' said Smart Alec.

What do you call a school jacket that's on fire?
   A blazer.

Teacher: 'Who can tell me what 'dogma' means?'
Cheeky Charlie: 'It's a lady dog that's had puppies.'

Which capital city cheats in exams?
   Peking.

Teacher: 'Eat up your roast beef, it's full of iron.'
Dottie: 'No wonder it's so tough.'

Dad: 'Would you like a pocket calculator for your birthday, son?'
Son: 'No thanks, Dad. I know how many pockets I've got.'

Teacher: 'Who can name four members of the cat family?'
Silly Sue: 'Mother cat, Father cat, and two kittens.'

Polly: 'Is it true that before we are born we are dust, and after we are dead we are dust?'
Teacher: 'Yes.'
Polly: 'Help! There's someone under my desk and I don't know if he's coming or going!'

Mr Fearsome, the teacher, took his secretary, Miss Prim, out for lunch. As the waiter approached their table he enquired abruptly, 'Do you serve crabs here?'

'Yes, Sir,' replied the waiter, holding up his pad and pencil. 'In this restaurant we serve everyone!'

Why is it dangerous to add up in the jungle?
Because if you add four and four you get ate.

Anne: 'Did you hear what happened to poor Mr Wally's wavy hair after his accident?'
Dan: 'No, what happened?'
Anne: 'It waved goodbye.'

Jake: 'Our new teacher has lots of money, but apparently his house doesn't have a bathroom.'
Blake: 'Why's that?'
Jake: 'Because he's filthy rich.'

Knock, knock.
Who's there?
Luke.
Luke who?
Luke through the keyhole and you'll see me.

TEECH SUDDENLY FEELING TIRED

Knock, knock.
Who's there?
Pencil.
Pencil who?
Pencil fall down if the elastic snaps.

Teacher: 'Can you spell your name backwards for me, Simon?'
Simon: 'No, Mis.'

What's purple and 4000 miles in length?
  The Grape Wall of China.

How could a French chef revive someone suffering from school dinners?
  By giving them the quiche of life.

Geography teacher: 'Can anyone say what is the coldest place on earth?'
Mary: 'Chile.'

Teacher: 'Martin, didn't you hear me call you?'
Martin: 'Yes, but you told me never to answer back.'

Dance teacher: 'You'd be a wonderful dancer if it weren't for two things.'
Phillip: 'What's that?'
Dance teacher: 'Your feet!'

Where can you dance in California?
San Fran'disco.

The first form was having a party, but Dopey Dick didn't want to go. His teacher asked him why not. 'Well, Miss,' he replied, 'the invitation said from four to six – and I'm seven.'

What's the definition of a good actor?
    Somebody who tries hard to be everybody but himself.

How many times can you subtract 17 from 149?
    Only once, because after that you are not subtracting it from 149.

Why did the English teacher marry the school caretaker?
    Because the caretaker swept her off her feet.

What were the only creatures not to go into the Ark in pairs?
    Maggots. They went in an apple.

Why was the caretaker unhappy with his job?
    Because he believed that grime didn't pay.

PILE IN THE DESERT BY HOOFLUNG DUNG

What did Noah do when it was dark?
    He switched on the floodlights.

What did Johnny say when he found his school dinner was a plateful of beetroot?
    'That beet's everything.'

Teacher: 'Who can tell me the name of the man who invented gunpowder?'
Danny: 'It must have been someone who wanted guns to look pretty, Miss.'

Teacher: 'What was the Romans' greatest accomplishment?'
Smart Alec: 'Learning Latin!'

Knock, knock.
Who's there?
Norma Lee.
Norma Lee who?
Norma Lee I go to school every day.

Why did the teacher stand on her head?
    So she could turn things over in her mind.

What's the hardest thing about learning to ride a bike?
    The ground.

Teacher: 'Edward, take 100 lines!'
Edward: 'Where to, Miss?'

What steps do you take when the headmaster is on the rampage?
Very big ones!

Proud mum: 'Our Monica learned to play the violin in no time.'
Music teacher: 'Yes, I've often heard her playing like that.'

Proud mum: 'Do you think my daughter should take up the violin as a career?'
Music teacher: 'No, I think she should put down the lid as a favour.'

Dottie: 'It's awful, Miss. Everybody thinks I tell lies.'
Teacher: 'I don't believe you.'

Why did the PT teacher wear two pairs of trousers when he played golf?
   In case he got a hole in one.

Teacher: 'When do kettles have scale?'
Jimmy: 'When they sing instead of whistle.'

THE HILLS ARE ALIVE WITH THE SOUND OF MUSIC!!

Teacher: 'What's in the middle of March?'
Clever Clara: 'The letter R, Miss.'

Why did the pupil go to night school?
  To learn to read in the dark.

Teacher: 'Who was that on the phone?'
Samantha: 'No one important, Miss. Just some man who said it was long distance from Australia, so I told him I knew that already.'

Teacher: 'You're wearing a very strange pair of socks, Darren. One's blue with red spots, and one's yellow with green stripes.'
Darren: 'Yes, and I've got another pair like it at home, Sir.'

Geography teacher: 'What is the Cheddar Gorge?'
Susie: 'Er, a thick cheese sandwich, Sir?'

Harry: 'Please may I have another pear, Miss?'
Teacher: 'Another, Harry? They don't grow on trees, you know.'

Chemistry teacher: 'What is H_2SO_4?'
Miranda: 'Oh, er, it's on the tip of my tongue.'
Chemistry teacher: 'Then you'd better spit it out quickly, because it's sulphuric acid!'

What's the very lowest game you can play?
   Baseball.

Arthur: 'Mrs Smith, our history teacher, is married to a fireman.'
Martha: 'Really?'
Arthur: 'Yes, and every year for Christmas he puts a ladder in her stocking.'

Teacher: 'What is an oyster?'
Smart Alec: 'It's what firefighters shout when they have to lift a heavy woman out of a burning building.'

Teacher: 'Who was the first woman in the world?'
Class: 'Don't know.'
Teacher: 'Yes you do. Remember the story of the apple?'
Soppy Sarah: 'Was it Granny Smith, Miss?'

Clever Dick: 'I've thought of a way of making the cricket team more successful.'
PT Teacher: 'Good. Does that mean you're leaving it?'

What did Smart Alec say when the school bell fell off its tower?
Someone dropped a clanger!

GOOD JOKE EH!

History teacher: 'What was the first thing Elizabeth I did on coming to the throne?'
Selina: 'Er, sat down, Miss?'

Biology teacher: 'What kind of birds do we get in captivity?'
Janet: 'Jail birds, Sir.'

Maths teacher: 'If you bought sixteen buns for 32p, what would each bun be?'
Clever Dick: 'Stale, Sir.'

Teacher: 'Emma, why won't you enter the long jump competition?'
Emma: 'I'm allergic to sand, Miss.'

Teacher: 'Now, Clara, give me a sentence with two pronouns in it.'
Clara: 'Who, me?'
Teacher: 'Correct.'

English teacher: 'Can you give me a sentence using the word 'fascinate'?'
Clara: 'My raincoat has ten buttons but I can only fasten eight.'

Teacher: 'Who was Cleopatra?'
Gemma: 'She was Queen of Denial, Miss.'

What must you pay when you go to school?
Attention!

Teacher: 'I see you don't cut your hair any longer, Nigel!'
Nigel: 'No Sir, I cut it shorter.'

'But Mum, I don't want to go to school today. Please don't make me!'

'But, Clarence, you must go. You're the teacher!'

Science teacher: 'Who can name a deadly poison?'
Smart Alec: 'Hang gliding.'
Science teacher: 'What do you mean, hang gliding?'
Smart Alec: 'One drop and you're dead!'

Teacher: 'Why weren't you at school yesterday?'
Marie: 'Please, Miss, I was sick.'
Teacher: 'Sick of what?'
Marie: 'Sick of school!'

Teacher: 'What's your name, boy?'
William: 'William.'
Teacher: 'Say 'Sir' when you speak to me.''
William: 'All right, Sir William.'

Teacher: 'What have you heard about the Dead Sea?'
Maureen: 'I hadn't even heard it was ill, Sir.'

Knock, knock.
Who's there?
Gladys.
Gladys who?
Gladys Friday, aren't you?

How do dinosaurs pass exams?
   With extinction.

Pupil: 'Have you been at school all your life, Sir?'
Teacher: 'Not yet, Jenkins.'

Why did the composer spend all his time in bed?
   Because he wrote sheet music.

How does an intruder get into school?
   Intruder window.

Teacher: 'What do we mean by 'horse sense'?'
Smart Alec: 'Stable thinking, Miss.'

Teacher: 'How old are you, Lucy?'
Lucy: 'I'm not old, I'm almost new.'

Teacher: 'Trevor, wipe that sulky look off your face immediately! What would you say if I came into class with a face like that?'
Trevor: 'I'd be too polite to mention it.'

Art teacher: 'I asked you to draw a horse in a field, but you've only drawn the horse.'
Smart Alec: 'That's because the horse has eaten all the field.'

What's the most magic lesson in school?
  Spelling.

Aspiring Angie: 'I'd call my drawing a rare work of art.'
Art teacher: 'I'd agree it isn't well done.'

A teacher took her class for a walk in the country and Susie found a grass snake. 'Come quickly, Miss,' she called. 'I've found a tail without a body!'

Pupil: 'Miss, my pen's run out.'
Teacher: 'Run after it then.'

Why wasn't the artist short of money?
    Because he was always drawing cheques.

How do teachers dress in January?
    Quickly.

KNOCK KNOCK –
WHO'S THERE?
TEACHER.
TEACHER WHO?
TEACHER!!

GULP! RUN FOR IT LAD!!

Art teacher: 'What colours would you paint the sun and the wind?'
Paul: 'The sun rose and the wind blue.'

'Teacher, teacher, can you help me out, please?'
'Certainly! Which way did you come in?'

When is a blue school book not a blue school book?
When it is read.

Why did the teacher sleep on a saddle?
In case she had nightmares.

When is an English teacher like a judge?
  When she hands out long sentences.

Laugh and your friends laugh with you, but you stay in detention alone.

Teacher: 'Who signed the Magna Carta?'
Stanley: 'It wasn't me, Miss.'

Mandy: 'Our teacher went on a banana diet.'
Andy: 'Did he lose weight?'
Mandy: 'No, but he could climb trees really well.'

Alec's class went on a nature study ramble.
'What do you call a thing with ten legs, red spots and great big jaws, Sir?' asked Alec.

'I've no idea. Why do you ask?' replied the teacher.

'Because one just crawled up your trouser leg!' said Alec.

If a teacher fell off a step-ladder, what would she fall against?

Against her wishes.

Why did the teacher sleep under the bed?

Because he thought he was a little potty.

If ten teachers and ten pupils stood together
under an umbrella, why wouldn't they get wet?
    It wasn't raining.

Alec: 'Do you say seven and three is eleven, or
seven and three are eleven?'
Alan: 'Seven and three are eleven.'
Alec: 'No they're not. Seven and three are ten.'

Teacher: 'Dennis, when you yawn you should put
your hand to your mouth.'
Dennis: 'What, and get it bitten!'

When does a teacher become two teachers?
    When she's beside herself.

Teacher: 'What is the shortest bridge in the world?'

Smart Alec: 'The bridge of your nose.'

Teacher: 'Do you realise it takes two sheep to knit one jumper?'

Claire: 'I didn't even know sheep could knit!'

SHEEP CAN DO LOTS OF THINGS!

Teacher: 'What can anyone tell me about Toulouse, in France?'
Clever Dick: 'Everyone there has two bathrooms, Sir.'

Teacher: 'Mary, why were you late today?'
Mary: 'I overslept, Miss.'
Teacher: 'You don't mean to tell me you sleep at home as well?'

Teacher: 'Who can give me a word meaning the opposite of minimum?'
Kate: 'Minidad, Sir?'

What did the pencil say to the rubber?
    'Take me to your ruler.'

Teacher: 'William, you've been studying French for five years and you're still bottom of the class. When are you going to get ahead?'
William: 'Please, Sir, I've already got one.'

Careers master: 'Now what kind of job do you think you would like, James?'
James: 'One with plenty of openings.'
Careers master: 'How about being a doorman?'

Teacher: 'What do we mean by a 'bee line'?'
Clever Clara: 'A line between two buzz stops.'

THAT JOKE GIVES ME A BUZZ!

Teacher: 'Who can tell me where King Solomon's Temple was?'
Kitty: 'On his forehead, Miss?'

Why did the school pencils go on strike?
    Because they were all suffering from leadaches.

Nigel: 'You said the school dentist would be painless, but he wasn't.'
Teacher: 'Did he hurt you?'
Nigel: 'No, but he screamed a lot when I bit his little finger.'

Barney: 'Shall I tell you the joke about the pencil?'
Brian: 'No, there's no point to it.'

Why is a drama teacher like something out of the Wild West?
   Because she's a stage coach.

Why is a classroom like an old car?
Because it's full of nuts and has a crank at the front.

Teacher: 'I hope I didn't see you copying just now, Susan.'
Susan: 'I hope you didn't either, Miss.'

Science teacher: 'Can you tell me one substance that conducts electricity, Jane?'
Jane: 'Why, er...'
Science teacher: 'Wire is correct.'

Geography teacher: 'How can you prove that the world is round?'
Ben: 'But I never said it was, Sir.'

Maths teacher: 'Are you good at arithmetic?'
Linda: 'Well, yes and no.'
Maths teacher: 'What do you mean, yes and no?'
Linda: 'Yes, I'm no good at arithmetic.'

Bill: 'Who was the fastest runner in history?'
Jill: 'Adam. He was first in the human race.'

Teacher: 'Tell me ten animals that come from Africa.'
Linda: 'Nine lions and an elephant.'

Vicky's English teacher called on her at home.
'May I see your mother?' asked the teacher.

'She ain't in,' replied Vicky.

'Vicky, where's your grammar?' exclaimed the teacher.

'She ain't in, neither,' replied Vicky.

Teacher: 'Who knows what 'unaware' means?'
Barbara: 'It's the first thing you put on in the morning, Miss.'

If the maths teacher faints, what number does she need?

You should try to bring her 2.

Teacher: 'Why are you always late?'
Roger: 'I threw away my alarm clock.'
Teacher: 'But why did you throw away your alarm clock?'
Roger: 'Because it always went off when I was asleep.'

Teacher: 'How many letters are there in the alphabet?'
Paul: 'Eleven, Miss.'
Teacher: 'Why do you say eleven?'
Paul: 'Well, there are three in 'the' and eight in 'alphabet'.'

School doctor: 'Have you ever had trouble with appendicitis?'
Roger: 'Only when I tried to spell it.'

Charles: 'What do you call a baby ladybird?'
Chrissie: 'A little humbug.'

Why did the teacher's sister give up her job in the biscuit factory?
    Because it was driving her crackers.

Teacher: 'Who knows what a shamrock is?'
Jimmy: 'It's a fake diamond, Miss.'

FOR THIS - JIMMY WOS BEATEN LIGHTLY WITH AN IRON BAR!

History teacher: 'What was Camelot famous for?'
Ben: 'Its knight life.'

A black and white cat crossed Alec's path. For the rest of the day his luck was decidedly patchy.

Teacher: 'What's the difference between a buffalo and a bison?'
Cockney Clare: 'You can't wash your hands in a buffalo, Miss.'

Teacher: 'Put your coat on, Alec, the barometer's falling.'
Smart Alec: 'Obviously it wasn't properly fixed to the wall.'

Clever Dick: 'Have you ever seen a catfish, Sir?'
Teacher: 'Yes, I have.'
Clever Dick: 'How did it hold the rod?'

Why should a school not be near a chicken farm?
To avoid the pupils overhearing fowl language.

The class was out on a nature ramble. 'What a pretty colour that cow is, Miss,' exclaimed Julie.

'That's a Jersey, Julie,' replied her teacher.

'Oh, really, Miss?' said Julie. 'I thought it was her fur.'

The PT teacher was trying to teach Weedy Willie to box. Weedy Willie hadn't managed to land one punch on his opponent.

'Keep swinging, Willie,' urged his teacher. 'The draught might give him a cold.'

What do you get if you cross a school burglar with a cement mixer?
A hardened criminal.

Two girls were talking in the corridor.
'That boy over there is getting on my nerves,' said Jennifer.
'But he's not even looking at you,' replied her friend.
'That's what's getting on my nerves,' grumbled Jennifer.

How do you count cows?
    With a cowculator.

What's black when clean, and white when dirty?
    A blackboard.

How did Dim Donald get a burnt ear?
    He said he was listening to the match.

Polly had worked very hard at her gymnastics
and her teacher could tell that she was very tired.
'Why don't you take the bus home instead of
walking?' suggested her teacher.
    'Because if I did my mum would only make
me bring it back,' sighed Polly

Teacher: 'Who can tell me what a zebra is?'
Molly: 'It's a horse with venetian blinds, Miss.'

Horace: 'Old potato peelings, tin cans, used envelopes, chicken bones...'
Teacher: 'Horace, stop talking rubbish!'

Fred: 'I keep thinking I'm invisible.'
Teacher: 'Who said that?'

Teacher: 'There were three apples in my drawer this morning, and now there's only one. Why is that?'
Dennis: 'I guess the last apple must have been hidden at the back.'

Cheeky Charlie: 'Have you got *Who Killed Cock Robin*?'
Librarian: 'Who is it by?'
Cheeky Charlie: 'Howard I. Know.'

If you put Alec and his friends in a London Underground train, what would you have?
    A Tube of Smarties.

Teacher (in a cafe): 'Can I have a coffee, please, without cream?'
Waiter: 'We're out of cream. Will you have it without milk?'

Samantha sat yawning in class. 'Why are you yawning in class?' asked her teacher.

'Please, Miss, I don't sleep very well,' she replied.

'Try counting sheep,' said her teacher.

'I did,' answered Samantha. 'I got to 4,236,786 and it was time to get up.'

Bob: 'John just swallowed his pen, Sir.'
Teacher: 'Then tell him to use a pencil.'

Did you hear about the teacher who dreamed she was eating a giant marshmallow?

She woke up and her pillow had gone.

Barney: 'I keep seeing double, Sir.'
Teacher: 'Sit down at your desk, Barney.'
Barney: 'Which one, Sir?'

What's the difference between a well-behaved dog and a poor scholar?
One rarely bites, the other barely writes.

What did the Eskimo children say when their teacher was leaving?
   'Freeze a Jolly Good Fellow.'

Sheila: 'I don't think I deserve a nought for my English test.'
Teacher: 'Neither do I, but I couldn't give you a lower mark.'

Wayne: 'Our teacher fell out of her bedroom window yesterday.'
Jane: 'Did he hurt himself?'
Wayne: 'Not really. He lives in a bungalow.'

Geography teacher: 'What is a Fjord?'
Clever Clara: 'A Norwegian motor car, Miss.'

What do you call someone who shouts loudly at a soccer match?
   A foot-bawler.

Mrs Smith and Mr Brown were chatting about why they entered the teaching profession. 'I used to be a fortune teller before I became a teacher,' said Mrs Smith. 'But I had to give it up. There was no future in it.'

Miss Jones was out shopping. 'I'd like a dress to wear around the classroom,' she said.
   'Certainly, madam,' replied the shop assistant. 'How big is your classroom?'

Mr Greenfinger, the botany teacher, was a keen gardener. On his day off he spent from early morning to late evening digging at his vegetable plot. Alec watched him. 'You've been digging all day, Sir,' he said. 'What are you growing?'

'Extremely tired!' replied Mr Greenfinger.

Jenny: 'Why do you have three pairs of glasses, Sir?'
Teacher: 'One for distance, one for reading, and one pair to look for the other two.'

A teacher was helping her sister in her grocer's shop one day. The teacher was 1.7 metres tall, and she took size 6 shoes. What did she weigh?
Bacon and cheese.

What exams are horses good at?
    Hay levels.

Teacher: 'How far away from school do you live, Tony?'
Tony: 'Five minutes' walk if you run, Sir.'

NEWSFLASH: A large hole has been discovered in St. Mary's School playground. Engineers are looking into it.

What's the difference between a gymnastics teacher and a duck?
   One goes quick on its legs, the other goes quack on its legs.

When is ink like a pig?
   When it's in a pen.

Playground teacher: 'What happened when Humpty Dumpty fell off the wall?'
Clever Dick: 'All the king's horses and all the king's men had scrambled egg for breakfast.'

What do you get if you cross a caretaker and a bad-tempered teacher?
   Is there a difference?

The English teacher was telling the maths teacher about his sister's wedding. 'She married an Irishman, you know, and has gone to live in Tipperary,' said the English teacher.

'Oh, really?' said the maths teacher.

'No, O'Reilly,' corrected the English teacher.

NEWSPAPER ADVERTISEMENT:

'School teacher's house for sale in Cornish fishing village. Three bedrooms, dining-room, kitchen, sea-through lounge.'

How did Vikings communicate with each other?

By Norse code.

HOI SVEN! — HUTZ ZÜCTE GOTHJUTLK BLOODINK!

Larry: 'Do you remember Jenkins, that prefect who was a karate champion?'
Barry: 'Yes, why?'
Larry: 'He joined the Army, but he had to leave.'
Barry: 'Why was that?'
Larry: 'Every time he saluted, he ended up in hospital.'

History teacher: 'Who invented Sir Arthur's Round Table?'
Smart Alec: 'Sir Cumference.'

Knock, knock.
Who's there?
Bernadette.
Bernadette who?
Bernadette all of my sweets.

Sign outside the school caretaker's hut: Will the person who took my ladder please return it, or further steps will be taken.

Why is a school caretaker nothing like Robinson Crusoe?
    Because Robinson Crusoe got all his work done by Friday.

What do you get if you cross a caretaker with a monk who smokes large cigars?
    A caretaker with a bad habit.

Teacher: 'Who invented the radio?'
Smart Alec: 'Was it Macaroni, Sir?'

What did Alec say when Allen shot towards him in the archery class?
    'That was an arrow escape!'

What does the music teacher do when he's locked out of the classroom?
    Sing until he gets the right key.

Why did the school football team
players a lighter?
    Because they kept losing thei

The cook
nuts fo
sh

Teacher: 'What was the highes
Great Britain before Ben Nevis w..
Debbie: 'I don't know, Miss.'
Teacher: 'Ben Nevis, of course!'

Teacher: 'Why do monkeys swing in the trees?'
Smart Alec: 'Because there aren't any swings in
the jungle.'

When Jimmy went swimming and all his clothes
were stolen, what did he come home in?
    The dark.

ery teacher was in a delicatessen buying
the afternoon's cake baking.

'What kind of nuts would you like?' asked the
op assistant.

'Cashew,' replied the teacher.

'Bless you,' said the shop assistant. 'What
kind of nuts would you like?'

*What kind of musical instrument can you use
for fishing?*
The cast-a-net.

Knock, knock.
Who's there?
Sacha.
Sacha who?
Sacha lot of questions in this exam.

Where did Noah keep his bees?
   In the Ark hives.

Teacher: 'Do you like opera, Francesca?'
Francesca: 'Apart from the singing, yes.'

Teacher: 'Who knows the story of *Puss in Boots*?'
Smart Alec: 'I know! It's about a cat in a chemist's, Miss.'

Teacher: 'Does anyone know what parrots eat?'
Smart Alec: 'Polyfilla, Sir.'

I'M PLASTERED

Music student: 'Did you really learn how to play the violin in six easy lessons?'
Music teacher: 'Yes, but the 500 that followed were pretty difficult.'

Music teacher: 'Where is Paul?'
Peter: 'He's still in the music room playing a piano duet. I finished first.'

Why is it difficult to open a piano?
Because all the keys are inside.

Why did the music student have a piano in the bathroom?
Because he was practising Handel's Water Music.

Teacher, on nature ramble: 'Now take care not to fall into the pond, children. It's over two metres deep.'
Silly Susie: 'But, Miss, it only reaches up to the middle of those ducks!'

Teacher: 'A pork chop, please, and make it lean.'
Dinner lady: 'Certainly, Mrs Smith. Which way?'

Did you hear about the Scottish teacher who washed his kilt?
The next day he couldn't do a fling with it!

Naughty Nicky: 'Did you hear the story about the dirty shirt?'
Teacher: 'No.'
Naughty Nicky: 'That's one on you!'

Science teacher: 'What kind of food do pelicans like to eat?'
David: 'Anything that fits the bill, Sir.'

Teacher: 'What is cowhide used for?'
Silly Sarah: 'To hold cows together.'

Teacher: 'How can you catch a squirrel in your garden?'
Smart Alec: 'Climb a tree and act like a nut.'

Music teacher: 'Cynthia, why are you standing on that step-ladder?'
Cynthia: 'So I can reach the high notes, Miss.'

Three teachers went out in the rain, but only one got his hair wet. Why?
    The other two were bald!

Smart Alec: 'Have you got holes in your socks, Sir?'
Teacher: 'Certainly not!'
Smart Alec: 'Then how do you get them on your feet?'

What do you get if you cross your least favourite teacher with a telescope?
A horrorscope.

Why did the bald teacher throw away his keys?
Because he no longer had any locks.

What always starts with a tie?
A three-legged race.

Why was Alec's brother thrown out of the submarine service?
    Because he liked to sleep with the window open.

Rude Ruth: 'I think your new suit fits you like a glove, Sir.'
Teacher: 'Do you really think so?'
Rude Ruth: 'Yes, it's a pity it doesn't fit you like a suit!'

Gymnastics teacher: 'I'll make you all so strong that you'll be able to tear up telephone directories.'
Smart Alec: 'That's nothing. My brother often runs out of the house and tears up the street.'

Susie: 'Is it safe to swim on a full stomach?'
Sally: 'It's much safer to swim in water.'

When Alec went round collecting for the new swimming pool for his school, someone gave him a large bucketful of water!

The maths teacher and the English teacher went out for a quick pizza after school. 'How long will the pizza be?' asked the maths teacher.

'Sorry, Sir,' replied the waiter. 'We don't do long pizzas, just round ones.'

Why was the student witch so bad at essays?
Because she couldn't spell properly.

Teacher: 'How many famous people were born during Roman times?'
Smart Alec: 'None, Miss, they were all babies.'

Did you hear about the teacher who found a fly in her soup? She said it must have committed insecticide.

Knock, knock.
Who's there?
Phyllis.
Phyllis who?
Phyllis in on the latest news.

Knock, knock.
Who's there?
Ida.
Ida who?
Ida nawful time at school today.

What did one classroom wall say to another?
    'I'll meet you at the corner.'

If a person suffered from water on the knee, how would Alec cure him?
    He'd make him wear drainpipe trousers.

When is the water in the shower room musical?
    When it's piping hot.

Alec complained to the school cook that there was just one small potato on his plate. 'Just a minute,' she said, 'and I'll cut it in two for you.'

Why did the mean teacher walk around with her purse open?
She'd read there was going to be some change in the weather.

Maths teacher: 'How did you find the weather on your Scottish holiday, Melissa?'
Melissa: 'I just walked outside, Miss, and there it was.'

Gemma: 'Our teacher went to the West Indies for her holiday.'
Emma: 'Jamaica?'
Gemma: 'No, she went of her own accord.'

Two science teachers were having a discussion. 'Did you know that someone has discovered how to make wool out of milk?' said the first teacher.

'Goodness,' replied the second, 'that'll make the cows feel sheepish!'

Sarah: 'Did you hear about Samantha now she's left school? She's working for a company that makes blotting paper.'
Selina: 'Does she enjoy it?'
Sarah: 'I believe she finds it very absorbing.'

Teacher: 'Now, children, you must all have seen a window box at some time.'
Clever Clara: 'I've seen a garden fence, Miss.'

Teacher: 'Why are you crossing the road at this dangerous corner? Can't you see there's a zebra crossing just a little further on?'
Pupil: 'Well I hope it's having better luck than I am, Miss.'

What's the best part of going on a school trip?
   Going home.

What kind of job is easy to stick to?
   Working in a glue factory.

Why do some people want to become teachers?
So they can be in a class of their own.

Why is it hard work being a physics teacher?
Because they all have so many ions in the fire.

When George left school, he said he was going to be a printer. All the teachers said he was just the right type.

There were ten giraffes in the zoo. All but nine escaped. How many were left?
Nine!

At Christmas the school went to a special service in church. The teacher asked if they had enjoyed it, and if they had behaved themselves.

'Oh, yes, Miss,' said Brenda. 'A lady came round and offered us a plate full of money, but we all said no thank you.'

Several of his friends believed Alec would make a great plasterer when he left school. You see, whenever he told a story, he always laid it on good and thick.

Teacher: 'What do we mean by an inkling?'
Ronald: 'A baby pen, Sir.'

Teacher: 'Do you think insects are intelligent?'
Kevin: 'Well, wasps always seem to know when we're having a picnic, Miss.'

Linda wanted to be a singer when she left school. She sang at an amateur concert and was thrilled by the way she performed.

'Oooh,' she cooed to her friends, 'did you hear the way my voice filled the theatre?'

'Yes,' replied one, 'and did you notice how the audience left to make room for it?'

Caspar: 'I was the teacher's pet last year.'
Jaspar: 'Why was that?'
Caspar: 'She couldn't afford a dog.'

Teacher: 'Who was Ivanhoe?'
Emma: 'A russian gardener.'

Teacher: 'What's the most common illness in the Far East?'
Jamie: 'Kung flu.'

What's the best way to avoid being troubled by biting insects?
    Don't bite any!

Selina: 'What is an ig?'
Jim: 'An Eskimo house without a loo.'

What kind of umbrella does a teacher carry on a rainy day?
A wet one.

Why did the teacher fix her bed to a chandelier?
Because she was a light sleeper.

Is a teacher's life worth living?
That depends on the liver.

Teacher: 'Where is your exercise book, Lynne?'
Lynne: 'I ain't got one, Miss.'
Teacher: 'Don't say 'ain't', say 'haven't'. I haven't got my exercise book, you haven't got an exercise book, they haven't got any exercise books.'
Lynne: 'Gosh, Miss, what's happened to all our exercise books?'

Angus: 'How were your exam questions?'
Fergus: 'They were OK, but I had trouble with the answers.'

Mrs Smith: 'What is your son going to be when he's passed all his exams?'
Mrs Brown: 'At the rate he's going, I'd say a pensioner!'

Did you hear what happened when Simple Simon tried to swim the Channel? He got tired two miles from the French coast, so he turned back!

Smart Alec went on a camping holiday with the school.
   'Did the tent leak?' asked his brother.
   'Only when it rained,' replied Alec.

On the same trip, Alec's friend Jimmy went fishing. He was sitting beside a sign that said 'NO FISHING' in large capital letters, when a gamekeeper appeared.
   'Oy, you!' called the gamekeeper. 'You're not allowed to fish there!'
   'I'm not fishing,' replied Jimmy. 'I'm teaching my worms to swim.'

Teacher: 'Brian, why do you always fail your exams?'
Brian: 'Because you always set the wrong answers, Sir.'

Teacher: 'Who can tell me what an octopus is?'
Jenny: 'It's a cat with eight legs, Miss.'

To whom does every teacher take his hat off?
   His barber.

Why did the teacher call both her children Ed?
   Because she thought two Eds were better than one.

WOULD YOU MIND TAKING YOUR HAT OFF?

THAT'S NO HAT! THAT'S MY HAIR!

Why was the teacher not pleased when he bumped into an old friend?

Because they were both driving cars at the time.

Why did the school orchestra have bad manners?

Because it didn't know how to conduct itself.

Why do some teachers put their hair in rollers?

To wake up *curly* in the morning.

Why is it unusual for a teacher to wear dark glasses?

Because the class isn't usually bright enough for her to need them.

The class went to a concert. Afterwards Jackie asked the music teacher why the members of the orchestra kept looking at a book while they played. 'Those books are the score,' replied the teacher.

'Really?' replied Jackie. 'Who was winning?'

Teacher: 'Does anyone know what guerilla warfare is?'
Smart Alec: 'Monkeys throwing nuts at each other.'

The games teacher had broken off her engagement. The science teacher asked her what had happened. 'I thought it was love at first sight,' said the science teacher.

'It was, but it was the second and third sights that changed my mind.'

Knock knock,
Who's there?
Victor.
Victor who?
Victor his shorts in the football match.

Did you hear about the boy who was so lazy he went round with his mouth open to save him the trouble when he wanted to yawn?

*What did the teacher say on the school trip
to France?*
    'Every time I get on a ferry, it makes me cross.'

Teacher: 'Simon, what are you so angry about?'
Simon: 'It's all the rage, Miss.'

Teacher: 'Where does satisfaction come from?'
Smart Alec: 'A satisfactory.'

How does a teacher get through life with no teeth?
    She just grins and bears it.

What does a teacher lose every time she stands up?
    Her lap.

Teacher: 'Write 'I must not forget my gym kit' 100 times.'
Bob: 'But, Sir, I only forgot it once!'

I MUST NOT FORGET MY GYM KIT
I FUST BUT NORGET MY PIM TWIT
I BUST KOT NORFLETCH MOR TWERP TIP
I KNOWT BIT NOT SCHNIDS MY STITCH TIT
201 PLUM BOTS TROLIP MOI TWIT FLIT
EEUUGH · I FEEL ILL!!

Teacher: 'Recite your tables to me, Joan.'
Joan: 'Dining-room table, kitchen table, bedside table...'

Teacher: 'What are the best shoes made from?'
Janet: 'I don't know, but bananas make the best slippers!'

Knock, knock.
Who's there?
Quiet Tina.
Quiet Tina who?
Quiet Tina classroom.

Teacher: 'Why are you always late in the morning, Steve?'
Steve: 'Because you always ring the bell before I get here, Sir.'

Teacher: 'What's a robin?'
John: 'A bird that steals, Miss.'

Why was the schoolboy such a slow swimmer?
    Because he could only crawl.

Among the books in the school library are:
Fishing for Beginners by Rod N. Line
Heat and Light by Alec Tricity
Kidnapped by Caesar Quickly
A Bump on the Head by Esau Stars
Cheap Dinners by Tina Katzfood

Arthur: 'Did you know our PT teacher was an amateur boxer?'
Martha: 'Really?'
Arthur: 'Yes, they call him Leonardo Da Vinci.'
Martha: 'Why do they call him that?'
Arthur: 'Because he spends most of his time on the canvas.'

What did the painting say to the wall?
'First they framed me, then they hung me.'

Teacher: 'What stands in the middle of Paris?'
Pat: 'The letter R, Miss.'

Why did the teacher put a sticking plaster on her pay cheque?
Because she'd had a cut in her salary.

Teacher: 'What does impeccable mean?'
Eve: 'Something that birds won't eat.'

Teacher: 'Tell me something that is important today that didn't exist 200 years ago.'
Smart Alec: 'Me!'

Monica fancied herself as an artist, but her teacher said she was so bad it was a wonder she could draw breath.

Teacher: 'If 'can't' is short for 'cannot', what is 'don't' short for?'
Daft Dinah: 'Doughnut, Sir?'

Teacher: 'Put this sentence another way: *Her beauty was timeless.*'
Albert: 'Her face could stop a clock.'

Teacher: 'Who can tell me what language they speak in Cuba?'
Sammy: 'Er, is it Cubic, Miss?'

More books in the school library:
Fitted Carpets by Walter Wall
In the Woods by Theresa Greene
Winter Clothes by Mahatma Kote
Selling Old Cars by Con Allday
Old Junk by Heidi Hole

Teacher: 'Why are you late, Albert?'
Albert: 'My bike had a puncture, Sir.'
Teacher: 'Did you stop to mend it?'
Albert: 'No, I just raised the seat.'

Knock, knock.
Who's there?
Barbara.
Barbara who?
Barbara black sheep, have you any wool?

THAT JOKE MAKES ME FEEL SHEEPISH!

Stephen asked Alec if he could share his sledge.
'OK,' said Alec. 'We'll go halves.'
    'That's great,' said Stephen.
    'I'll have it downhill and you can have it uphill,' continued Alec.

Even more books in the school library:
How to Make Money by Robin Banks
Little Fishes by Anne Chovy
Guard Dogs by Al Satian
Wet Paint by Honor Park-Bench
Vertigo by Eileen Dover
Your Money or Your Life by Stan N. Deliver

Teacher: 'Can anyone give me a sentence using the word 'infamy'?'
Molly: 'They've all got it infamy, Miss?'

Teacher: 'What is the outside of a tree called?'
Class: 'Don't know, Miss.'
Teacher: 'Come on, yes you do. Bark, children, bark!'
Class: 'Woof, woof!'

Teacher: 'Who can tell me what a draughtsman does?'
Sally: 'Leaves doors open, Sir.'

Teacher: 'In which battle was Nelson killed?'
Smart Alec: 'His last one, Miss.'

I'LL TURN A BLIND EYE TO THAT!

Smart Alec: 'Did you hear about the idiot who goes around saying 'no'?'
Teacher: 'No.'
Smart Alec: 'So it's you, is it?'

Knock, knock.
Who's there?
Alaska.
Alaska who?
Alaska for another piece of cake.

Why are fish well educated?
    Because they live in schools.

How does a school salad say Grace?
    'Lettuce pray.'

Sally: 'Help! There's a little caterpillar in my salad.'
Dinner lady: 'Would you like a bigger one?'

What did Wilfred say when the chemistry teacher started to tell him off?
     'Ammonia little 'un!'

Science teacher: 'Who knows what zinc is?'
Clever Dick: 'It's where you wash ze dishes.'

Knock, knock.
Who's there?
Harmony.
Harmony who?
Harmony times must I tell you not to do that?

Teacher: 'Who can give me a sentence with the word 'bulletin' in it?'
Avril: 'He shot a bulletin the air, and whither it went he knew not where.'

Knock, knock.
Who's there?
Una.
Una who?
Unaforms are worn at our school.

Teacher: 'What kind of flower does a frog like?'
Anne: 'A *croakus*, Miss?'

Teacher: 'You must know what 'illegal' means?'
Angela: 'Er, a sick bird of prey, Miss?'

Cookery teacher: 'What are the signs of iron deficiency?'
Smart Alec: 'Crumpled shirt and trousers, Miss.'

Why did the school bus get a puncture?
    Because of the fork in the road.

Dad: 'Well, William, how many questions did you get right out of 100?'
William: 'All of them, except 99.'

Teacher: 'Why would you like to be a teacher, Clarence?'
Clarence: 'Because I wouldn't have to learn anything, Sir. I'd know everything by then.'

Teacher: 'I'd like a room, please.'
Hotel receptionist: 'Single, Sir?'
Teacher: 'Yes, but I am engaged.'